Home Business Ideas For

Women Of All Ages

By Kaye Dennan

ISBN-13: 978-1492225829

CONTENT

Introduction

SECTION 1 – About Being In Business

- Advantages Of A Home Based Business
- Disadvantages Of A Home Based Business
- Income: Is It A Business Or A Hobby
- Understanding Business Basics
- Your Home Business Environment
- What Skills Do You Have To Develop Further For Business
- What Contacts Can You Take Advantage Of
- Down To Business
  - What Type Of Business To Start
  - Business Plan And Research
  - Marketing Your Business
  - Website Development
  - Branding Your Business
- Outsourcing Help
- Transitioning To A Home Business

SECTION 2 – All About Choosing A Business And About Selling Your Product Or Service

INTRODUCTION

As mentioned in my bio I have had many years as a business owner, the past 12 years as a home business owner with 7 of these working on the internet. It is with my experience as a small business owner, then a home business owner and 6 years marketing on the internet **that puts me in a unique position to help home business owners** overcome some of their operational problems and how to get exposure on the internet, especially if they wish to sell internationally.

Home Business Ideas For Women Of All Ages has been written to give you an overview of what you need to consider when starting a home business.

In *Home Business Ideas For Women Of All Ages* I will firstly look at the basics of starting and running a business and then I will take you through a process to help you look at various types of home business ideas, from service businesses to home made products to …. Well anything you like really.

I will talk 'products' in this book but in actual fact I am usually referring to **both products and services.**

Managing and running a business basically uses the same methods to be successful, it is just the product that changes and just about everything I talk about can be adjusted to suit your business: service or product.

Let's look at how you can start your own business at home.

SECTION 1

Advantages Of A Home Based Business

Being self employed carries huge flexibility as you experience the freedom to make your own decisions and come and go as you like. Of course, in saying that, you cannot just breeze around the place without putting in the hours of work and expect to have a successful business.

One in thirteen people today are opting to become self employed and of those, over half of them are women. However, self employment also offers a great number of challenges, which you have to handle and we will look at some of those further on.

Below Are Different Benefits Of Being Self Employed:

You are your own boss

Being self employed can be regarded as the biggest advantage as you are working independently. There is no need to listen to blunt orders and unpleasant remarks from the boss. Now you are the one who is the focal point of your business, you enjoy supreme authority and can make all the decisions. But be careful, as being a boss you will carry the same essence of challenges and responsibilities as your boss had.

Work from home

If you are a self employed home business owner you can enjoy the comfort of your home and work in a relaxed atmosphere. This is one of the greatest advantages of being self employed, as you can work freely with no strict timings or dress code. You can choose a special corner and make it your workplace to keep files and business items. You can easily carry  your laptop to any place inside your home or you can even go outside and enjoy the good weather while you are working if your business allows that sort of mobility.

If you are making products then you have the flexibility to access your work all through the day if necessary and this can be very helpful to some who are making their own products, like candles, for instance.

Greater self satisfaction

As you are self employed and have no one sharing your business, you are the sole operator and can feel proud of yourself with the successes you achieve. There is no one who can become a partner of your success or claim to be the reason of your success. This type of self satisfaction comes when you create your very own goals and make specific decisions. It is one of the greatest advantages and feelings of satisfaction from being self employed.

When you do reach these heights with your business your next point of satisfaction will be from earning the income that you desire.

Manage your success

As you are the only one responsible, the chances of success are in your hands. The advantage of this is that you can put in the time and research to your business and know that it is done properly or to the best of your ability. When you follow on with a project you can be confident that everything you can think of has been put into it.

If something is going wrong you can get on to it straight away, not having to wait for decisions from 3 or more steps up the ladder before the matter can be rectified. This relates to the products and services themselves, but **also very importantly** any advertising campaign you are running. Larger companies can take up to 12 months to go through the meeting process to change decisions whereas a solopreneur can make instant decisions and often benefit from those decisions immediately by putting into practice a campaign to take advantage of a current trend.

You will take the responsibility of any failure and you will be the only one to claim profit and take credit when you become successful – the risks attached to being self employed are also great.

Constantly judge your product and your potential and enjoy the advantages of being self employed.

Work plan

Once you have an independent business you can exercise all the advantages of being self employed. You can create your own database of clients and choose those people with whom you want to work. There is no need to feel uneasy while dealing with unpleasant people as you would if you worked for someone else.

You set your work hours and days to suit you, your lifestyle and your desired income and you can set your holidays to suit.

Family flexibility

Ask any mother how disappointing it is to miss those special moments when their kids are at school and are being rewarded for their achievements or are in school plays or excelling on the sports field and they cannot get there.

When you are a work at home business owner you can plan these moments ahead and make sure that you are free to attend these special events. Not only do you benefit from it but so do your children.

Also if the children have after school activities you can be there to transport them so that they do not miss out on those activities.

Getting to appointments with the family is so much easier too because when you work for a boss it is so difficult to get time off to take kids to doctors, dentists and the like. If you have

sick children you are there at home with them so no-one has to miss a day or two's pay taking time off to care for them.

Stress levels are hugely reduced because when two parents are working away from home and not getting back til late in the afternoon or early evening the

parents can so easily get stressed when there is a traffic hold up or other incident that forces them to be extra late. When one person works at home life is so much easier.

For those women who do not have children at home a huge advantage for them is that if they set up a business online they can travel the country but still be able to work and make an income. How fantastic is that!

I am a grandparent of three young ones, 4, 6 and 8 and my husband and I love being able to attend their schools activities and we adjust our working hours so that we can babysit them regularly. My daughter's friends think she has it just too easy! Years ago I thought I would be in a shop front type business when she had children but when I turned my hand to having home businesses I realized my dream of being able to help with the children.

Meals can be attended to through the day as well if you need a break from your work. Say you have been working for 4 or 5 hours straight on your business you can go and prepare dinner to have a change of pace and a change of thought. Doesn't that make the evenings run so much smoother? You bet it does!

Disadvantages Of A Home Based Business

If you are pondering over the idea of starting a business at home, then you would want nothing less than be able to get the business up and functioning at its best. However, you might experience a few mistakes on your part during the initial phase, but with the eagerness to learn from them you will overcome them. Also, with enough in-depth analysis, you can easily avoid the most common pitfalls that most emerging entrepreneurs tend to make initially.

Following is a rundown of 9 of the most common problems faced by new home business owners:

Lack of proper planning: When starting a business at home, it's important to plan well ahead to overcome any possible difficulty, such as unexpected expenses or curtailment of supplies due to short supply or out of stock, etc. Unfortunately, some start up home businesses do not back their actions with proper future planning, and thus have to face the consequences if something goes wrong. Business/financial software such as Peachtree or Quickbooks not just helps you manage your budget, but they also allow you to plan out your future income potential and expenses well in advance.

No budget: Because a home business owner does not have one of the larger expenses of running a business, commercial rent, they often tend not to keep to a strict budget and even worse, do not open business accounts to keep all transactions separate. This is one of the very first steps you should take once you have decided to start a business. You want to keep all your business transactions separate right from the very first payment. Budgeting a home business is made even worse by the fact that when you are at home you are always being tapped up for more money for the odd family expense. Cash businesses especially experience difficulty here. What happens then, is that when you have to purchase something for the business, you are out of funds. Not a good situation.

Unable to save money for annual bills: Account management is one of the most common pitfalls of any home based business and running out of cash earlier than expected and having nothing with which to pay those annual bills is a common problem for the inexperienced. So, it is important that you consult experts and take their opinion on key areas such as minimizing taxes, saving enough cash in the bank as well as forecasting your initial costs. Getting your finances and budgets right before you even open the doors is a critical part of keeping those doors open in the long term. You need to know:

- how much it will cost to set up
- how much it will cost to run until you make a profit
- how much to upgrade any equipment or purchase more as your business grows
- how much you can spend on marketing
- what other expenses that you may run into as your business grows

Lack of a professional place for client meetings: Unless you have devoted a self-contained portion of your house to the business, it's not really a good idea to meet your clients or business associates at home. Sad but true- it may cause an adverse effect on your image and credibility. So, in the absence of a proper meeting place, it's always recommended that you hold your meetings at any off-site place – such as a coffee house or restaurant or any decent neutral venue with a favorable environment for conducting business meetings.

Legal constraints: Before proceeding ahead with starting a business at home, it is really important that you study the zoning laws, permits, licensing and any other legal obligation you will be required to take care of. After all, the last thing you would ever want is to do is lay out all the plans, buy your equipment, arrange everything and announce that you are open for business, only to find out that the existing laws make it illegal to operate your type of business out of residential premises.

Maintaining a professional image: Some people have the perception that a home business is being run as a hobby and that the service will be below standard, so to ensure that your business does not give that impression, you need to have a professional 'front' for it, covering every aspect of business management. The only way to alter their perception in your favor is by giving the impression that you have your own business site by printing business cards, subscribing to a separate phone line for your business, getting a post office box for mail and taking any other possible measures to project a professional image.

It is always recommended that you subscribe to a dedicated business phone line, or at least keep a cell phone exclusively for taking your business calls. Frequent phone calls from your friends and family can often unwittingly eat up your precious business hours, so a phone line which is separate from your  personal number is a basic necessity for all start ups. This way you can put your home phone on message and keep your business line for business. This is a very good tip for improving your business time management.

One of the main ways in today's world of technology, of making your business look professional is to have your own active website whether you sell from it or not.

Time management: However, the above problems are not the only ones you are likely to face when beginning your new home business – in fact there will be plenty more, such as having to answer the door time and again, the children in the house storming into your workplace and most commonly, the lure for that seemingly irresistible afternoon break for 10 minutes which ends up being 45 minutes with the feet up watching TV.

This is where your self-discipline will need to come in. A drop in income will soon have you wondering about what you are doing with your day if you are starting to take the lazy option. (Of course, lazy is only if you are meant to be working! Taking planned time for leisure is not being lazy, it is being sensible.)

Not enough space for work: This is another common problem that most emerging entrepreneurs face when starting a business at home. Unless you have abundant funds, then it's more likely that you will find yourself cramped alongside your desk, file cabinets as well as other essential office necessities in a corner of your bedroom or basement. Worse even, if you are selling goods from your home then chances are high that sooner or later the inventory will pile up to almost an unmanageable level. Unfortunately, there is no magical solution to get yourself out of such a mess– it all depends upon your ability to make the best use of the space you have available and your management skills so ensure that you plan accordingly. There are ways around this by using half a garage, putting up a shed out back or using a spare bedroom, but do keep all this in mind when you start out.

Many a good business has started in the corner of the lounge or bedroom, or even in the kitchen for that matter, so keep in mind it is not where you are working but the image your portray to your customers and your focus on self belief that you will be able to work your way out of that situation if you really want to.

Stress relief: Starting a business at home may sound fun as well as an epitome of self-reliance and independence because you will be your own boss, but remember, it may also backfire on you at times by making you feel lonely and stressed. So, it is important that you learn to balance your personal and professional life. Work is important, but distancing yourself from fun and family can do more harm than good in the long run. Separate your working times from your personal life and **give quality** time to both.

Lack of self-discipline: Your productivity as a home based worker may drastically improve or reduce depending upon your willpower and self management skills. Starting a home based business means you will always be your own boss so it is important that you instil a good work ethic right at the beginning. You don't want to end up in the situation of having no code of conduct to follow; no formal routine that you must stick to everyday and above all, no daily, weekly or monthly target to meet.

If you cannot maintain a certain level of control over your daily actions, the consequences upon your new business may not be all bright and shiny. After doing all the hard work in setting up a new business, you certainly won't want to lose it all because of your laziness or lack of self discipline.

Once you make the commitment to start a business stick to it and give it your very best.

Be prepared to go through thick and thin to make your business work. The fact of life is that running a business does not go smoothly and there are times when you wonder why on earth you are bothering to keep trying. But believe me most business owners face the same problem of lack of motivation during difficult times. Work through your problems and just keep at it to come out the other end, so to speak.

No business was built in a day and no business went in a straight line from new to successful.

Income: Is It A Business Or A Hobby?

I won't spend much time on this topic because essentially it is all covered as a collective in the book, but I just want to make sure you realize the difference between a **hobby** and a **business.**

A **business** is where you engage in activities to make a profit and a **hobby** is an activity you do for fun.

One point to consider is if you are going to turn a hobby into a money making concern, and many do, then you need to make sure that you are costing your products and overheads correctly. A point that often does get overlooked when a hobby is turned into a business is that the operator tends to overlook costing in their time.

I don't know where you live but make some enquiries if you need to and find out what the basic hourly rate is for a similar job. That is what you need to cost into your product or service. In saying that, you may decide that your hourly rate is not worth the full rate initially until you can streamline your business somewhat and get the work done faster. Be careful with that calculation.

It really is quite difficult to work this out on some homemade products.

If you do your sums and feel that you just cannot make a product that gives you the hourly rate, plus materials cost, plus overheads, then you need to seriously think about whether you should be doing it for the business. I am talking from experience here and you are the only person who can make these decisions. I know when I was not making a lot of money, but doing art work, I was happy to take a lower income for a couple of years because I had been in a stressful business for some years and I thought a couple of years doing something creative would be wonderful, and it was and I don't regret it.

But whatever business you plan on doing the costing of your product or service is one the most important aspects to get right for the survival of the business at ground level.

If you are making product as your chosen business then ensure that you will always be able to get your materials whenever you want them, especially leading up to your prime selling times. If you are making something that larger companies also make materials can at times be sold out.

You might like to visit my Home Business Success website and read more about costing homemade products:

http://homebusinesssuccessideas.com/costing-your-homemade-products/

Remember: it is always best to price higher and reduce the price than it is to have a low price and no room to go down for promoted sales or weekly specials, or whatever it is that you intend to use to attract business.

Understanding Business Basics

There are a lot of steps that need to be taken to set up a business and a lot that needs to be put into practice during the running of the business.

In all of those, once the business is set up, the main issues that a home business owner needs to focus on are:

- keeping your focus and staying committed for the long term
- managing the finances of the business at all times
- providing a quality product or service
- growing your customer base and keeping in touch
- costing your product or service correctly and reviewing periodically
- marketing your home business

That list is really all encompassing in some ways as each issue in itself contains more than one action. But if you keep those issues under control you have a very good chance of having a successful business.

Your Home Business Environment

Your home business environment includes both the physical area and the emotional environment. As mentioned earlier you will have to consider where you are going to operate the business from at home and this will be determined by the type of business you will be operating and the availability of space, and perhaps even such necessities as power or internet connections.

As for the emotional environment you need to be aware of what is happening as regards the impact on the family.

This alone covers many issues depending on:

- the age of children
- the freedom you have to run your business
- the activities that need to take place for the business to run successfully
- any help or hindrance that you are going to get from the family
- the attitude of your partner or other people you may live with
- the necessity of your business to provide X amount of dollars towards the family income and what the resulting emotions will be if that is not achieved
- the time that you need to give the family in any given week

- whether you have a partner at home full time who may want their space
- if you are a carer for a family member
- your own health and the health of others

What Skills Do You Have To Develop Further For Your Business

When you are a sole operator of a business you have not only responsibility for, but often have to actually do, everything pertaining to the business, such as:

- having original business ideas
- making sure the income is earned
- making sure bills are paid on time and expenses kept under control
- marketing your products
- selling your products
- keeping watch on your competition
- bookkeeping and tracking sales of different products and services (this is not the same as just paying bills and is much more time consuming but very important information)
- cleaning up your work area
- writing your blog
- sourcing materials
- purchasing

You can see that this is quite an endless list so when you are considering what more you need to learn for your business take into account that at some stage as you grow your business you will most likely need to have the odd part-time person to manage some of the above tasks. That is usually the only way a one person business operation can grow, by outsourcing some of the work or employing someone to come in and help. There are lots of women out there who are happy to be involved for a few hours a week but who do not want the commitment of a business. They may be able to help you.

If you feel that you need to learn some new or more advanced skills for your business then I would suggest that if at all

possible you get that training out of the way before you start your business. The first months of starting a business is quite time consuming and it is difficult to take on anything else like education.

There is a lot of training that can be done online so that can be very helpful if you can download audios and videos because you may be able to listen and train yourself while you working, depending on what it is you are doing.

The sub-conscious mind is an amazing thing and if you have never trained yourself this way before you will be amazed at what you can take in while you are actively doing your job, i.e., depending on the concentration you need for your job.

What Contacts Can You Take Advantage Of

When setting up your business you need to think of everyone you possibly can to whom you can tell about your business. Everyone from the mechanic to the school teacher and beyond!

You need to perfect an **Elevator Speech**. This is known as a quick 2 minute breakdown of your business because usually that is all the time you have 'in an elevator' should someone ask you what you do for a living.

There are many instances as you move through your week where you can give your 'elevator speech' such as at the bank, in an elevator, at the local coffee shop, school or bakery, so make sure you have one and that you remember it.

To put an elevator speech together you need to think about exactly what you do and the service you provide and why you do it and then put all that into a quick sentence or two.

Mine is:

"I am an author of Home Business and Lifestyle books which I sell on Amazon and I also have websites supporting these books."

Other examples:

"I make gel candles and specialize in designs for weddings and parties. I also sell them wholesale through gift shops."

"I have my own unique range of wooden children's toys made with organically grown wood and stained with natural products which I sell online."

Down To Business

Below is a list of what you have to do to get your business up and going.

- Decide What Type Of Business To Start
- Write A Business Plan And Do The Research
- Write A Marketing Plan For Your Business
- Decide On Your Website Development
- Branding Your Business

Outsourcing help

Now I know that as a one person business or a small home business operator you often feel like a one armed paper hanger, and that of course is where much of the stress can come from when you are a solopreneur.

At times you may decide to get some help with your workload. Locally you can get people to help with bookkeeping and the like but online you can outsource through various sites. These outsourcing sites are excellent for getting blog writing, graphic design, sales scripts, admin support, and finance support done which can take an immense load off your mind. The prices are very good and usually the delivery is reasonable as well.

One point I would just mention here is that often times when you feel you need help is when you are growing your business and at a financial point when you are just starting to make a profit and you feel that if you get help you are not going to have any profit again. This is one of these unfortunate steps to growing a business. It is like taking three steps forwards and one step backwards.

But as long as you keep taking those forward steps you will come out on top in the end. If you don't take this backwards step (financially that is) then you will find that you will not grow, or even worse will burn out and just throw your hands up in the air and say, "enough is enough, I'm out of here." Don't let that happen it is just one of those growing pains that you have to go through and is why I say that you need to choose something you like doing so that you keep focused on the end outcome.

To help you with your marketing and keeping your blog up to date you can outsource some or all of the work.

Personally, I not only have my home business coaching site HomeBusinessSuccessIdeas.com, but before I started setting that site up I spent 6 years learning about internet marketing and during that time have set up over 30 websites from which I sell information products.

I DO KNOW that I am not superwoman so I outsource a lot of my articles!

I have them written and tweak them for my personal purposes then either put them up on my sites or use them for placing in article directories for article marketing.

Here is a rough guide as to how to go about placing your work on outsourcing sites (be aware though that each site has its own system):

- put up your job (be as specific as possible so that you get what you want using detailed instructions and give your keywords – look at others to see how their job descriptions are worded)

- wait to receive proposals from candidates
- compare the replies and view portfolios
- select the one that you wish to work with

The one tip that I would give you here is to make sure that you are getting articles written with good English grammar and spelling because if you put poor quality work up on your site it will do you more harm than good.

We all make typos and we all miss the odd mistake here and there but the work **must be easily readable and it must be informational**. Don't accept anything that is below par.

And the bonus is that you can always add your own little bit to make it more personal and add information that the writer may not know about. It is just that getting the basic article written you don't need to spend as much time on it, time you often don't feel you have. I tend to work about one month ahead with my writers and this way I do not feel under pressure at any stage with my blogging due to having nothing ready. It does not matter if written copy sits on my computer for weeks. I would rather that than have nothing ready when I am under pressure with my business.

Then again if you wish, you can get someone to do the whole internet work for you if it is not something that you want to do. These people are called 'virtual assistants'.

Outsourcing sites that you can look to have work done for you is:

- Elance.com
- Craigslist.com
- Fivver.com
- ODesk.com
- Freelancer.com

There are many other sites and you can find them on Google by searching for 'outsourcing sites'.

Virtual Assistants will do your writing, your blog posting, all your social marketing and any other work you want done. Of course, there is a cost to this so it is something you would need to budget for.

Transitioning Into Your Home Based Business

If you are working and plan on having a business at home then it is a good idea to transition into your home business while you are still at work. Let's say you plan on retiring from the work force and want to have a home based business to earn some extra income. It would be a good idea to do all your background work as mentioned in Section 1 before you leave work. Even if you are going to have a long holiday when you finish, it is still best to get all that work behind you while you are working because it is time consuming and not income producing.

Another benefit of that is once you decide on what you want to do your mind starts focusing on that and it is amazing how you will see ideas associated with your choice well before you even start your business.

Take for example when you are going to buy a new car. Once you have decided how much you want to pay and then decide on a make and model you will be amazed at how many of that type of car you will see on the road. At least double what you ever saw before!! Why? Well all of a sudden you are focusing on that model car and your mind has subconsciously decided to see every one there is. This is called the **'power of attraction'**... what you focus on you will receive.

SECTION 2

All about choosing a business and about selling your product or service

Because there are so many options here I have had to think long and hard how to present it to you in the best way so what I am going to do is run through the starting points that everyone will have and then I have grouped some jobs types together at the end.

How To Choose What To Do

There are several factors here that are very important and you will have to decide which is the most important to you. Making that final decision on what business to start will require you looking at a number of facts to see that it will produce the end result that you are after.

Here are the **three most important questions** that you need to take into account when making your final decision. You will need to work out **which is your first priority** and then make sure that the business you choose will allow you to fulfill that priority otherwise you will feel stressed each and every day due to feeling guilty.

1. Will I be able to earn the amount of money per month that I need from this type of business?
2. How soon will I need to generate an income?

3. Will I be able to work at home and take care of the children (or whatever other commitment you may have)?

Is your business choice something that you can see yourself working at for years to come and something you really enjoy?

If no.1 and no. 2 are the most important then you need to be considering something where you know you will get paid for the hours you put in. It may mean that you have to have a business where you can cost in a certain amount of money for the hours you put in such as: hairdressing, house cleaning, consultancy, teaching, body massage, or have a business where you are assured of an income such as working with a client base you have had in a previous job. Or are you prepared to wait for the level of income until the business grows.

With no. 3, if you are going to have children at home with you when you are working then you need something where you can leave the work if you have to when caring for the children, or you may have them in some sort of care at times to give you some work time. Or if there is another reason, is that more important than the other two reasons or can you work with no. 1 alongside this reason.

Skills And Education

Start by looking at your skills. If you have not been in the workforce for a number of years do not be overly concerned about that because if you have been a mother let me tell you that in your organizing of the home you have developed some very essential skills for running a business. If you haven't worked for a while look at skills that you can learn and take classes if needs be.

The skills that you may have could be: computer skills, a hobby that could be profitable, bookkeeping, party planning, event management, specialist gardening, aromatherapy certificates, health and beauty knowledge, writing skills, or one of a host of other skills you may have.

What you should do is list down all your skills and then mark down from 1-10 how likely it would be for you to make money from each skill. Then when you have done that start eliminating the ones that you don't think would make a good business for you to run from home.

Running a home based business does not necessarily mean that you are at home all the time unless you choose a business that requires that commitment. For example, you might have a mobile dog washing unit. But your business would still be home based because that is where your 'head quarters' are and where you do all your phone, marketing and bookkeeping work.

If for example, you have a creative mind and good organizational skills you may start a business where you buy in t'shirts and design, or have designed, patterns to be printed on them and then manage the selling and distribution. This method for a home business is very wide ranging from crockery, through linen to whatever. You would probably need storage at home as well.

Part-Time Or Full-Time

First up let me say that 'earning' is not the same as 'takings'. 'Takings' is the money taken in sales of your products or service, and earnings is what is left after all your expenses have been paid.

As regards your income you need to focus on this before setting up too, because in most cases your hours of work and income are related to each other, especially at the beginning. There is no point in saying, "I want to earn $300pw, and I only want to work 10 hours a week." In some instances this could be possible, but unless you are sure that what you are going to choose allows you to earn $30 ph then there is no way you can have the two.

This then relates to whether you are going to be able to work part-time in the business and earn the $300 pw that you want or whether you need to focus on it being a full-time commitment.

Your Personality And How It Will Affect Your Business

Personality is something that a lot of people would never think about when it comes to setting up a business but let me tell you it is something that does play quite a major role on the success of your business.

I had a ceramic and folk art studio and I loved doing both, but when it came to the teaching I just did not have the patience and it showed. In the end I got some teachers in to do that work and I concentrated on selling the related products and making hand painted ceramic ware and started a party plan business with hand painted ceramics.

I am the sort of person who is a little introverted although I do love being with people and being involved in selling. I am a lousy teacher, correct that, I can teach quite well but I definitely do not like doing it and it shows. In a work situation I would rather get on with what I am doing and I love being hands on.

So when you are thinking about what you want to do have a good look at your personality and see how it will affect your business.

Also look at your decision making skills. If you cannot easily and quickly make decisions then you may be better to consider the type of business that runs with some sort of consistency rather than one where you are faced with making new decisions several times a day.

Family Commitment

Consider the family, its commitment to helping you either by being helpful or alternatively staying out of the way. If you do not have the backing of the family it can make life quite difficult.

Finances

Make sure you know your exact financial situation:

- Do you have the required funds to set up your business
- Do you have funds to see you through your personal expenses in the initial period when you may not be making a profit
- Do you have funds to run your business until it makes a profit
- Do you have funds to market your business

I beg you not to be blasé about your finances because if they are not right they will bring you down quicker than anything else and will cause you a great deal of stress.

In saying that there are certain types of businesses that can be set up with very little money but it is the keeping them going that you would need to focus on. Such businesses as: an eBay selling business, garden care, home care/cleaning, writing and the like where there is not much of an initial outlay.

Some business types would need continual upgrading of equipment, such as a garden care business.

Various Ways To Sell Your Product Or Service

Did you know that it is said that a person needs to be exposed to your product or service 7 times before they will buy! How does that make you feel? Probably a little despondent! But when you think about it if you know those facts then you won't get despondent until you have shown them 7 times, will you?

Of course, there are exceptions to the rule but when you look at your own buying pattern, think about how many times you look at new products before you buy.

There is a range of ways to sell products and when you are deciding on your business type give some serious thought to just how you can sell your product or service.

The internet is a huge forum but it is not for everybody. It is good for physical products, information products, online coaching or teaching, working for others online such as the virtual assistant, graphics designer, and so on.

If you are going to be selling locally look at wholesaling, and other ways that you can create interest in your product. Be prepared to do anything it takes to get your product out there when you first start out. Remember the '7 times to see it to make a sale' rule. That is how the successful people have had to start and it is the ones that stick with it through thick and thin that are the ones who win out in the end.

Before putting your product or service out there make enquiries, look around and see what your competition is up to, where they sell, how they sell and how they offer their specials. It is best to know all this before you start with your own business and that is one of the reasons why you do a business plan.

You can download a FREE **Business Plan Template** from our resources website: http://homebusinesssuccessstrategies.net/business-plan-template/

Managing Family Responsibilities And Your Business

The managing of family responsibilities needs to be given some thought and also some thought in relation to your desired income. I referred to that before about how many hours you will need to work to bring in the income that you desire.

Weigh all that up and if you go ahead with your business make sure that you have a strict working timetable so that you do give justice to both your business and your family.

In the next section is a long list of business ideas to consider. These suggestions are to open your eyes to the possibilities in the market place, but they may also trigger an even better idea that will suit you personally.

SECTION 3

Home Business Ideas To Consider

MAKING MONEY ONLINE

1. **Drop shipping** – having your own website promoting and selling products of another business but not being involved in the handling of the product, you are billed by the business for the product they send out and you make a profit on the price difference

2. **Ebay** – selling new and/or used products

3. **Affiliate marketing** – have your own website and sell products of another internet marketer through an affiliate marketing service like ClickBank and get paid a commission for the sale

4. **Mail order** – make or buy products which you stock and customers order off your website or from a booklet or flyer

5. **Virtual assistant** – working online helping other people or companies with their online requirements, there is quite a range of services which could be offered and you can have several clients when you run your own business

6. **Product reviews** – review products and get paid for doing so

7. **Surveys** – complete surveys and be paid for doing so

8. **Direct selling** – direct selling of products by various means such as by party plan, door to door selling, promotions with booklets, face to face sales

9. Social media posting – specialize in social media posting and offer your services to businesses (this could be part of a virtual assistance business)

10. **Blog writing** – become a blog writing specialist and write for other businesses
11. **Graphic design** – designing anything from logos, book covers, letterheads, business cards, flyers, etc. and you could have your own site and develop a business through an outsourcing company as well
12. **Website building** – if you have the knowledge you can build websites for clients
13. **Flipping websites** – building, promoting and then selling websites
14. **App development** – make apps for mobiles and iphones, etc.
15. **Selling ebooks at Amazon Kindle** – write books, reports or whatever you fancy and sell them on Amazon either as a physical book or as a Kindle book
16. **Product selling** – making and selling product on your own website and various other sites like eBay, Etsy, Amazon.
17. Work through an **outsourcing** company using your computer skills
18. Data entry – have work sent out to you and enter into company records
19. **Word processing** – typing up work for clients, building up your own client list

USE YOUR SKILLS

Some of these businesses will allow you to be paid by the hour or a set fee for the time that you put in and this does help plan your income. Whereas a business selling art works for example is one where you will never know from one month to the next what your income will be.

20. **Draughts woman** – drafting building designs
21. **Interior designer** – develop an interior design business working from home
22. **Business presentations** (put together) – plan and organize for clients
23. **Local guide** – be a local guide to show tourists around your area
24. **Accountant** – using your qualifications but work from home and actually do the work at home or spend some time out at client sites
25. **Bookkeeper** – do the basic bookkeeping for small business at home or spend some time out at client sites
26. **Freelance writer** – work for newspapers, magazines, and companies
27. **Author** – ebooks, books, magazine articles, poems
28. **Ad writing** – write ads for businesses on a freelance basis
29. **Artist** - create and sell online with your own website or through galleries
30. **Scrapbook artist** – make scrapbooks for momentous occasions such as weddings, births, anniversaries, sport events, etc.
31. **Craft artist** – make your own products and sell online, at shows, wholesale
32. **Diet coaching** – develop a client base of clients interested in good health
33. **Landscaping** – be a landscape artist, designer or worker

34. **Party and/or event planning** – organize parties, weddings, conferences and the like
35. Kids party planner/organizer – organize and manage kids parties
36. **Wedding photographer** – photography business specializing in weddings and can be incorporated with the videography as well
37. **Videography** – specialize in video work for clients such as conferences, etc.
38. **Photographer**
    - sell framed and unframed work of your chosen subject
    - sell online, i.e. Fotolia
39. **Flipping furniture** – sourcing used furniture, upgrading and selling
40. Home staging – become a professional home stager working with real estate agents, builders and construction companies
41. **Tour organizer** – organize tours for your area, you could have a range of tours that you promote and take a commission from the operators
42. **Tour operator** – have a tour that you host, something like bus trips, river cruises, skiing trips, whatever suits your area
43. **Home child care** - care for children in your home (this would need to be licensed)

CLASSES AND TUITION

There are a wide range of classes that can be taught either in your home or at other locations. Likewise these types of business will also give you a good indication of what your income is going to be.

44. Craft classes

45. Art classes

46. Fitness Instructor

47. Swim instructor

48. Tennis instructor

49. Tuition in chosen skill, e.g.
    - Music
    - Academic work

SERVICES

With a services business they can often be set up at very little cost and depending on what you are doing you are either working at home or away from home as a home based business.

50. Run errands

51. Shopping

52. Transcribing

53. Telemarketer

54. Beauty therapist

55. Hairdresser at home

56. Mobile hairdresser

57. Masseuse

58. Cleaner

59. Plant rental

60. Garden maintenance

61. Lawn care

62. Green housecleaning

63. Property manager

64. Courier

65. Household clearance

66. Home organizing

67. Errand business

68. Pet sitting

69. Mobile dog wash

70. Cartridge refilling

71. Safety training

72. Car wash

73. Mobile Cappuccino service

74. Mobile key cutting

LIFE SKILLS

Developing a client base of people who wish to get advice from you regarding the skills that you have developed:

75. Life coach
76. Career counseling
77. Financial planning
78. Stress management
79. Spiritual consultations
80. Mediation

MAKE

Below is a list of items as suggestions that you could make at home and sell. There are a number of ways to sell these items which have been described in the text in Section 2. Often times people who go down the path of making their own products find it difficult to make and sell so choose your method of selling that is not going to be too time consuming because you will need your time for the making of your product. These are good businesses if you have some support from family or friends. Sometimes two creative people can get together and share the selling which cuts down on that side of the business.

81. **Fishing flies**

82. **Clothing**

83. **Knitting**

84. **Crochet**

85. **Baby clothes**

86. **Sewer of unique items**

87. **Curtain making**

88. **Cake decorating**

89. **Specialty food provider**

90. **Cooking**

91. **Pastry cook**

92. **Healthy meals**

93. **Organic baby food**

94. **Gift baskets**

95. **Jewelry making**

96. **Candy making**

97. **Pickle range**

98. **Jam range**

99. **Homemade cookies**

100. **Party catering**

101. **Gift boxes**

102. **Linen range**

103. **Gift cards**

104. **Photo cards**

105. Unique stationery

106. Soft toys

107. Wooden items

- Toys
- Tables
- Kitchenware
- Household items
- Office items

TECHNICAL

108. Electronics repairer

109. Computer technician

PASSIVE INCOME

110. Share investing

111. Real estate rental property

Services Which Are Predominantly Done By Men But Women Are Also Being Involved And May Wish To Pursue As A Home Based Business

112. Plumber

113. Electrician

114. Car repairs

115. Car tuning

116. **Painter**

117. **Roofer**

118. **Concreter**

119. **Digger**

120. **House care – windows and gurney**

121. **Handyman**

122. **Gutter cleaning**

123. **Pool cleaning**

124. **Debt collecting**

Please note that these are suggestions only and many of them could be broken down into more specific business niches if you so wish.

Choose a business you would enjoy, research its possibilities, and write a business plan.

For further information and help on Home Based Businesses visit:

http://HomeBusinessSuccessIdeas.com

About the Author - Kaye Dennan

Kaye Dennan has been a small business for over 30 years.

Kaye started out very young as a business owner with over 35 staff. Over the years she enjoyed building and selling a number of businesses.

Some of those businesses have been a large catering business with 3 reception lounges (the first business), a franchise food store, a franchise business brokers office, several retail stores, human resources placement service and also art supplies with tutoring.

Over the past 7 years Kaye has been an online marketer as this is where she sees the future of marketing for all businesses, especially the smaller ones by being able to reach a wider audience.

Kaye believes that when she first started in business it was so easy to make money that it almost seemed like all you had to do was open your doors and you made a bucket load. But that is not the way it is today!

Today you have to plan, budget and promote like never before.

We live in a world of instant gratification. This is why it has now become imperative to have systems in place that make your customers think of you every time they want a product that is part of your range.

The thing is, if you know the basics of being a successful business owner you can use those skills to make any business successful.

To this end Kaye has written 5 books on small business with a view to helping new home business owners secure themselves in the market place.

Kaye was a **business broker for 6 years** and along with the experience gained there and the experience gained as a business operator for all those years, she has many hints, tips and strategies to share with you.

Kaye's home business website is Home Business Success Ideas: http://homebusinesssuccessideas.com

Disclaimer

The Publisher has striven to be as accurate and complete as possible in the creation of this book, notwithstanding the fact that she does not warrant or represent at any time that the contents within are accurate due to the rapidly changing nature of the Internet and financial controls.

While all attempts have been made to verify information provided in this publication, the Publisher assumes no responsibility for errors, omissions, or contrary interpretation of the subject matter herein. Any perceived slights of specific persons, peoples, or organizations are unintentional.

It is the responsibility of the reader to do their own research and seek advice from their business advisors.